La Clandestina

Luna de Salterain Valentone

BookLeaf Publishing

Presentation by *BookLeaf Publishing*

Web: www.bookleafpub.com

E-mail: info@bookleafpub.com

ISBN: 9789357212885

First edition 2023

To all the loves that have held me,

Thank you.

La Clandestina

This is the story of falling back into myself,
of holding the sky as it screams for rain,
clouds heavy and full.
This is the roar of the ocean
and the salt wind that kisses my cheek.
I miss you and forget you,
then find you
in the back corners of my house,
in crumpled notes,
in outgrown shirts,
in words I'd forgotten the taste of.
This is the housing of unhoused things,
this is the home I build
with empty hands.

Sundays for Posterity

I had all the intentions of
        cleaning the house today
of folding all the laundry,
    scrubbing the tub,
           of tucking away
           every
           dust bunny
     and shining the floors.
But instead,
    I found sunlight
        and the way it hit my face
        the way my eyes
           glow
        with the setting sun
   I found a memory of last night's dream,
        wispy and fragmented.
   I watched snow
        fall
and wondered
        whether
           the cat minds more
        being inside,
           or having wet paws.
I ate.
    Twice.

And finally,
  I vacuumed.
  Just vacuumed.
I opened the windows
    and the stale old air met
    the early morning breeze
  they said hello
  and danced in our kitchen
     and when I'd pass by,
  they'd leave me a kiss.
In the evening,
  you came home
  and we folded
     ourselves
  into each other,
     and slept, and
I realized that this too is for posterity.

Peaches and Plums

I have been thinking about peaches
     for three days.
Today,
     I walked two blocks in a
     rainstorm so strong,
       it soaked my shoes
         right through.
I called you,
     asking for a change of socks,
       and in twenty minutes,
      I see you with an umbrella
      and a bag tucked
        neatly
      under your arm.
There are fresh socks
     and dry sneakers,
     there is a thermos full of tea,
      a sandwich
        wrapped tight,
     and a peach.
The biggest,
     juiciest looking,
      most beautifully coloured peach
       in the world.
"I know you've been wanting,"

you said.

And I do not think that Williams' plums

could have been

as delicious

or sweet.

An Ode to a Town I've Yet to Know

I will get there,
              eventually.

We wait for the storm to clear,
              but she is fickle and full of rage.
        She does not take losing lightly,
              and tonight,
                  she loses hundreds.
We catapult through her,
                  seamlessly,
                  like rocks through fog
      and leave her,
              empty and alone,
                      to tend the
                      wounds
              of her soul
            ripped open.
    (distance means nothing
    for this kind of metal in flight)

Painfully upright, we sit
              and watch
              through rattling windows,

the unwavering gray close in on us,
            the horrifying display
                        of a shattering heart,
            a play we wish
                        we did not have to
                                    endure.

The sky is heavy with regret,
                a traitor in his own home.

His safe-carrying of us is a burden that
                refuses
                            to lessen
                                    with time.
        Despite this,
                we huddle before him
                            like children.
                "Take us home,"
                            we cry,
        but our pleas get lost in
                    lightning flashes,
                    in thunder,
                    in clouds so dense,
                    it feels as though we are
                moving
        through
concrete.

The marrow of our bones is electric now,

                              and an infinity
                                    later,
          our tired feet sink gently into new earth.

          The sky is inconsolable now,
                    attempts to return to the rivers
                                   every
                                        single
                                              drop
                    he once borrowed.

          The city stays solemn:
                         this grief is not hers to bear
                                        and through it,
                              she will keep us safe.
          "Things will be different in the morning",
                                        she says,
               "but only if you stay for it".

Pedestrian Eyes

A girl walks across oceans,
                     she picks balloons
           like flowers
               and they tether her
                   to the skies.
We slip fountain memories
       around the back of an old man's bike
       and wave goodbye
           across four lanes of traffic.
We walk 20 thousand steps to
                the yellow house,
    40 thousand steps across
               the sea and
                  into bed.
There are secret concerts that we stumble into,
      this is the candle-lit world that exists
                just for us.

Floral Fashions

Tucked away behind boxes,
            I imagine a ballroom
        full of ladies wearing
            flower dresses,
        their movement and depth
            unmatched
        by crinoline,
      or petticoats,
    or tulle.
Hours later,
you show me the twirl of a pink carnation,
        "look, it's dancing,"
           you say.

At home,
    you pull splinters
    out of my purple
        bleeding
         fingers,
    jabbing flower knives
        into flower wounds,
    and I wonder
      if
      this
      is not the way we become
        a rose.

Magnolia Blooms

This is honey-dripping love.
We move faster than we thought we could
                    and burned
            all the clocks
        we could find.
We tell time now by the
        sounds of shattering glass.
     (And yet,
        it cannot help but slip
        through our tired hands.)

Waste away with me,
          let's take the night bus
          to home feelings and
     I'll write you lists of what it means
            to piece
            this
            together.
These are puzzle fragments across time zones,
              continents,
          immense bodies
          of undrinkable water,
          and very
             slim
                odds.

I dangle my feet into oblivion,
       eat oranges
       like I will not eat again,
          and far off someplace,
     the day moon slips you secret notes.

We rearrange
     circadian rhythms
          to watch the sun
            wake up
   and now
       we refuse to close our eyes.
We've deciphered the horizon's screams,
     the burning orange
        turning
          sunset blue,
     the celestial bodies' attempts to
            at least
       whisper
   what they think about.

Find the pages of these thoughts
          pressing
the magnolia blooms we stole together,
       stole together because
         if they are everybody's,
       they are no one's,
       and really,
       how much could someone care.

For Josephine

I wonder about Peter Rabbit
             and his family
             in their burrow.
I wonder about his blue jacket
             with brass buttons.
             I wonder
                  if he knows
             it is a gift of labour.
I wonder about his mother,
             Josephine Rabbit,
      and how she puts her children to bed
      with a spoonful of
             chamomile tea.
      About the care she takes of her children.
         Stitching,
             washing,
                  mending,
        cooking,
             gardening,
             healing.
I wonder who takes care of her,
      who makes her dresses and aprons,
      who soothes her after a long day,
      who consoled
             the loss of her husband,
             or her son's

                              recklessness?
I wonder what was more gift,
              the onions and the
              found-again jacket,
              or
              her son.
I wonder
       if they admit this
       to each other.

An Ode to Vincent

With your turpentine tongue,
tell me about sunrises,
and sunsets,
and all of the flowers
that turned their faces
just
to say
hello
to you this morning.
Tell me about the most brilliant
yellows
and know
that i will love you
endlessly,
because
you
are.
How you sign your letters,
you will be:
ever mine.

El Equilibrio del Edulcorante

The room smells like sunrise and silk.
Sometimes,
it is so sweet
it's cloying.
Sometimes,
I add too much lemon
and I turn my sweets
sour.
Sometimes,
it's by accident.
Sometimes,
I'm just too scared of cavities.

Delicates

Cradle my moth heart in your hands -
who knew
how fragile this life could be -
a sugar castle world
sitting safely in
a snow globe.

What do you do when you find
a spider in your home?

I think we are
all
spiders
somewhere,
sometimes.

Even clothing needs protection
to be cleaned.
See how important it is then,
that we tread
gently.

A List

i. Stare and stare*
ii. Notice where people look
when they cross
a bridge
(it will almost always be
the water)
iii. Sometimes,
fireworks will fall into your
mouth.
Listen for the noises in your
tastebuds,
turn them into art and
lean into
what it feels like
to hear
tongues
dance.
iv. There will be
puddles of water
and
time travelling lines.
You decide
what that means
and
what to do with them.

v. You can converse with the furthest of stars,
they all have something to whisper,
listen.

vi. One day may

seem

far

away

but at some point,

so

did

today.

*you will see it eventually.

Tucking in the Sky

When the world is
      quiet
         and
            alone
and you ask for a story:
Every morning,
      the sun would scream,
    "come home, please come home",
and every night,
      the moon would whisper,
  "I am here".
But shooting stars
      never have been quick enough
        and messages always
     get lost
when it's cold.
          What I think
    I'm trying to say is that
        sometimes,
  we can't see the answer
even if we want it.

We Forgot to Set the Alarm

It is morning when we wake up
                              or not.
              We break fast first so it
                        must
              be morning.
The birds have been awake for hours,
                              or not,
          and the leaves of the orange tree
          are warm with sun.

A breeze blows
              gently
          through the cracks of our windows,
              it is the first we feel so it
                              must
                    be the morning
                        breeze.

The day fans out before us,
                    stretches lazily
                        and rolls over,
          shows us its fuzzy belly
                    and we pet it
                        vigorously.

There is little more delicious in this life
than the moments
we cannot find the start or end to.

(Lazy) Days

A pocket full of garden peas,
                and three days
        of doing none
                of what we planned.

I stare at the sky and
                notice all its different
                                shades of blue.
                They sear onto my eyelids,
                and for the next two hours,
                        all I know of is the
                                endless sky.
There are pink clouds,
                sitting deliciously
                in the distance,
                        and they invite me
                        to dive in.
How can you negate such a gentle coax,
                        such a sweet appeal?
I plunge,
        deeply,
                and forget what it feels like to
                have time
                        pass me by.

Road Maps

Body parts
    and credit cards,
            and all the ways we
                sell
                ourselves
        to get home.

You have been stranded for
                    six
            days,
        somewhere,
on the very
                    peripheries
        of your memory.

You know how to get back,
                somehow,
but it is hard to remember
                what you've forgotten.

Becoming and Returning

Weave the stars into your hair,
                   and
sear their glow into your skin
           because you came from them.
Every fibre in your body,
              a blend
              of love,
              cosmic dust,
              and good intentions.

Galaxies pierce through the electric suns
                  we leave on,
         to guide you home.

You came from them,
                  and to them
        you will return.
                Eventually.

A Well

I see you,
        carefully hiding
                hurricanes
           in the darks of your
              soul,
           in the dimly-lit alleys of your
              heart.

Perhaps it is worth now mentioning that
           no matter how many times
           you have been told,
                    near
                incessantly,
           that there is no use,
              for all that salt water
           you've so sadly
        accumulated
inside,
        bask
        now
           in the delicate rivulets
              that overboard your
                gleaming eyes.

And with whatever rests,

   you ingenious wonder,
move boldly,
   and use it to
put out the
raging fires
in your heart.

A Science Experiment

Nighttime is just the world upside down,
    let the leaves
        tickle your feet
    and the roots
        tangle in your hair.

There are mountain ranges
    that run along your spine,
        hiding
    between your blood and skin.

There are earthquakes
    that will shift your
        tectonic plates
    so many times over,
    you will begin to wonder
        if cartography
    was ever the way to go.

Board up your windows when you are
        feeling
        like this.

If you're lucky,
    you will see the stars.

They are angels driving by,
                    ask nicely,
          and they might
                    drop you off
                         at the moon.

A Home Grown Olive Grove

Paint me
softly
in orange,
adorn me with sunsets -
we are only
here
for a little while.

Dance with me as I come home,
It has been
two hours,
two days,
two months,
two lifetimes
without you.

Time exists outside of us now,
on a different plane -
4D movie theatres,
5D chess,
and us.

A wave, a scone, a laugh, a chair.
A home,
blue light,
a gentle beast,

                        a nest.
I offer you
            an olive branch
                        every time I undress,
            split gum,
            and cinnamon,
                and every shade of gold
                        you could imagine.

This is Orchestral and Growing

This is sunset blue,
    a sailor's daydream
        you're not sure
            you should stay up for.

An ocean sits in the middle of this park and
    you know you will lose your car here
        but there is a calm
    in these water sounds,
there is a loudness to be found in this quiet.

This is the first time I see you in the sun,
        and you wear daylight
          like it is yours
            alone.
You learn to walk through knee-deep snow
    to find me,
      follow convoluted maps of
        my foreign consonants
    to the yellow house
        and one day,
I would meet you there.

This is summer state delirium,

you knock on wood for me,
                tell of street fights,
        planetariums,
and travelling to the moon.

Esto es un juego del serio
                y hace años
                        que yo me vengo
                                preparando.

"This is orchestral and growing"
                This is what music looks like
                and
                this is just what it feels like
                                        when
                        I am with you.

This is a highway we cannot see the end of
                and a truck that hits and runs
                                and runs
                and runs.

I sleep on makeshift beds of gasoline tanks,
                we reconfigure death settings,
                                and I wonder if
                falling deep
                                        enough
                        means
coming out the other side.

This is realizing I'm not sure I'd mind anymore,
                    when your cinnamon
                              coffee
                    builds a home
          just like mine,
                    with shutters
               that work
     and
                         balconies
               that nearly don't.

We've learnt to distrust the weatherman now,
                         empty promises
                    sitting heavy
          on numb hands.
It is freezing and we still
               never know where to go,
          but worlds away,
                    we find the same things.
This is a dream
          I hate to hope you stay awake for.
This is a dream
          I hope you stay awake for,
                              and over there,
          I will meet you at the yellow house
                    and there will be sun,
               there will be sun,
          there will be sun.
There is so much beautiful light.

www.ingramcontent.com/pod-product-compliance
Lightning Source LLC
LaVergne TN
LVHW010935200726
843509LV00013B/2230